POSTCARD HISTORY SERIES

Lighthouses of the North Atlantic Coast

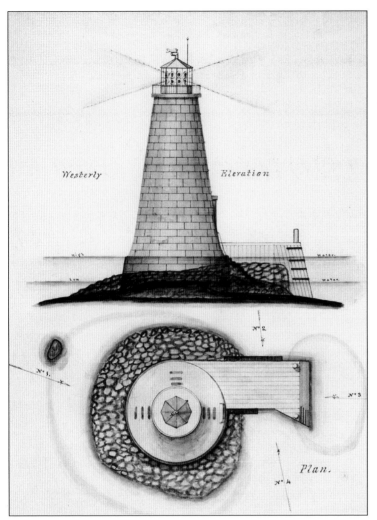

EXECUTION ROCKS LIGHTHOUSE, NEW YORK. In 1789, Congress passed an act for the establishment and support of lighthouses, beacons, buoys, and public piers. Two hundred years later, Congress passed a resolution designating August 7, 1989, as National Lighthouse Day. Seen here are the plans and elevation of Execution Rocks Lighthouse in New York in 1849. (Courtesy of the National Archives.)

Westerly   *Elevation*

Plan.

POSTCARD HISTORY SERIES

Lighthouses of the North Atlantic Coast

Linda Osborne Cynowa

ARCADIA
PUBLISHING

Copyright © 2023 by Linda Osborne Cynowa
ISBN 978-1-4671-6034-6

Published by Arcadia Publishing
Charleston, South Carolina

Printed in the United States of America

Library of Congress Control Number: 2023939490

For all general information contact Arcadia Publishing at:
Telephone 843-853-2070
Fax 843-853-0044
E-mail sales@arcadiapublishing.com
For customer service and orders:
Toll-Free 1-888-313-2665

Visit us on the Internet at www.arcadiapublishing.com

*This book is dedicated to all the historians and archivists who work so hard
to keep the many pieces of our past safe for future generations.*

*To the many lightkeepers, both men and women, who maintained the lights
in the lonely conditions and helped keep the lakes and seas as safe as possible
for navigation.*

Contents

Acknowledgments   6

Introduction   7

1.   Maine   9

2.   New Hampshire   37

3.   Massachusetts   41

4.   Rhode Island   69

5.   Connecticut   83

6.   New York   95

7.   New Jersey   111

8.   Delaware   123

Bibliography   127

ACKNOWLEDGMENTS

It is once again with the greatest appreciation that I thank Julie Oparka, a certified archivist and historian, for her research abilities, editing, and very importantly her photographic and technical support.

I would also like to mention and thank all the many places where more information on these very important lighthouses can be obtained: American Lighthouse Foundation, Delaware Bay Lighthouse Keepers & Friends Association, United Lighthouse Society, the Museum at Portland Head Light, Pond Island National Wildlife Refuge, Friends of Wood Island Lighthouse, Monhegan Historical and Cultural Museum Association, Friends of the Pemaquid Point Lighthouse, Friends of Seguin Island, St. George Historical Society, Acadia National Park, Friends of Swans Island Lighthouse, Franklin Island National Wildlife Refuge, Maine Lights Program, Kennebunkport Conservation Trust, West Quoddy Head Light Keepers Association, New England Lighthouse Lovers, Island Heritage Trust, Cuckolds Island Fog Signal and Light Station, Friends of Portsmouth Harbor Lighthouse (Whaleback Ledge Light), White Island State Historical Site, Save our Sankaty, Nauset Light Preservation Society, Beverly Historical Society, Friends of Plum Island Light, Thacher Island Association, Scituate Historical Society, Fort Pickering Light Association, Friends of Ned's Point Lighthouse, Friends of Nobska Light, Martha's Vineyard Historical Society, Beavertail Lighthouse Museum Association, Friends of Sakonnet Lighthouse, Rose Island Lighthouse Foundation, Dutch Island Lighthouse Society, Friends of Pomham Rocks Lighthouse, Norwalk Seaport Association, Stonington Historical Society, Green Ledge Light Preservation Society, Fire Island Preservation Society, Montauk Historical Society, Historically Significant Structures, Saugerties Lighthouse Conservancy, Athens Lighthouse Preservation Society, Sea Girt Lighthouse Citizens Committee, Hereford Inlet Lighthouse Commission, Friends of Barnegat Lighthouse, Maurice River Historical Society, and New Friends of Fenwick Lighthouse.

All postcards, unless otherwise credited, are the property of the author. The author can be reached through the website lindaosbornecynowa.com for more information. For further information on these important beacons of navigation, look into the many well-written and informative books by Jeremy D'Entremont.

INTRODUCTION

A lighthouse is loosely defined as a tower or structure used to display a light for the guidance of ships to either avoid a dangerous area, such as shoals or reefs, or to identify a safe harbor. The purpose of the light is to provide the ships at sea with a fixed point of reference to aid their ability to navigate in the dark when the shore or offshore hazards cannot be seen directly. The distance from which a light can be seen depends on the height and intensity of the light. The brighter the light and the greater its height above the sea, the farther it can be seen. These lights provide early warnings of reefs, sandbars, submerged rocks, and unseen cliffs and as daymarks and landmarks at night when fog, snow, haze, and wind whip up the sea itself.

Many hazards are encountered off the shores of the northern Atlantic states, where the lighthouses were so important. Its thick fog that settles over waterways in this area sometimes makes noticing hazards impossible, leading to this area being known as the "Graveyard of the Atlantic." Maine, New Hampshire, Massachusetts, Rhode Island, Connecticut, New York, New Jersey, and Delaware are the focus of this book, with vintage postcards showing what many of these states' lighthouses once looked like. Many of the buildings around the light stations have been torn down and removed, and in some places, only the light tower now exists.

Before the US Lighthouse Board was established in 1852, local collectors of customs were responsible for lighthouses in their area and worked under Stephen Pleasonton, who was known for his work in document preservation and his bureaucratic work in overseeing the Treasury Department's Lighthouse Establishment. The Lighthouse Board was in effect until 1910, when the US Lighthouse Service was created to take over lighthouse responsibilities. In 1939, Pres. Franklin Roosevelt decided to incorporate the Lighthouse Service and transfer it to the US Coast Guard. As their importance to navigation has diminished while public interest in them has increased, the Coast Guard has been turning over ownership and responsibilities for their running to individual societies, towns, and among others, the National Park Service, because of the expense of maintaining these structures. With the sentimental and historical attachment to these lights, a solution was needed.

The National Historic Lighthouse Preservation Act of 2000 created a process for the transfer of federally owned lighthouses into private hands. With the automation of the lighthouses early in the 20th century and a further push in the 1960s, the goal was to relieve most of the keepers. These high-maintenance structures are constantly subjected to ocean and lake air and the invasive effects of water and ice. Quite often, the land around the lights was lost to erosion. With the unmanned structures being left to the ravages of vandals and thieves, their automation led to their demolition and destruction. Many of the lighthouses are now under the protection of the National Register of Historic Places.

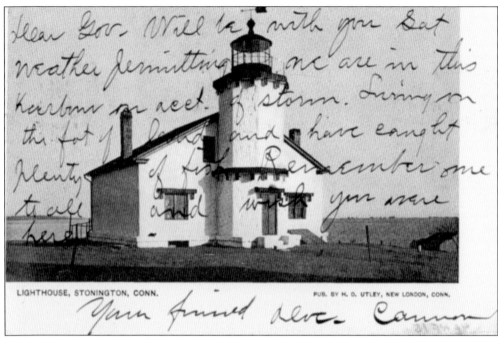

LIGHTHOUSE, STONINGTON, CONN.

PUB. BY H. D. UTLEY, NEW LONDON, CONN.

STONINGTON HARBOR LIGHTHOUSE, STONINGTON, CONNECTICUT. The Postal Act of May 19, 1898, provided for the extensive private production of postcards measuring 3.25 by 5.5 inches. Messages could only be written on the front, as seen here. The back was reserved exclusively for the address. After March 1, 1907, the law specified that messages could be written on the backs of cards. Cards of this new style were called "divided back" because of the vertical line to the left of which a message could be written, with the address on the right. "Undivided back" cards remained in the inventories of shops for many years.

One

MAINE

PORTLAND HEAD LIGHT, CAPE ELIZABETH, ME.   801

PORTLAND HEAD LIGHT, CAPE ELIZABETH, 1791. When completed in 1791, the original plans called for the tower of the Portland Head Light at Portland Point to be 58 feet tall, but during construction, it was raised to 72 feet. By 1813, it was lowered by 20 feet. In 1864, it was raised by 20 feet. In 1883, the tower was once again lowered by 20 feet. By 1884, after complaints, the light was once again raised by 20 feet, and a second-order lens fitted into the lantern room.

PORTLAND HEAD LIGHTHOUSE, CAPE ELIZABETH. In 1816, a new one-story 20 by 34 foot keeper's house was built of stone with two rooms, an attic, and an area for a kitchen. The original 1790 dwelling had become unusable. Because of inclement weather, there was a need for the keeper's area to be attached to the tower. In 1891, the stone keeper's house was taken down, and a wood-frame duplex 42 feet by 42 feet was built with room for both the head keeper and the assistant keeper. Over the years, many changes and improvements were made to the tower and the dwelling as weather pushed the limits of the structures. On August 7, 1989, The light was automated.

1926 July

POND ISLAND LIGHT, MOUTH KENNEBEC RIVER, ME 6

POND ISLAND LIGHTHOUSE, PHIPPSBURG. The towers and dwellings built in 1821, 1835, and 1843 had all seen the need for improvements. In 1855, a 20-foot tower made of a stronger brick was built and fitted with a fifth-order Fresnel lens, along with a wood-frame keeper's dwelling connected to the tower by a covered walkway. A new lantern was built in 1896, and the keeper's dwelling was given a much-needed renovation. In August 1960, the Coast Guard automated the light station. At that time, all the outer buildings were destroyed by the Coast Guard. In 1973, it became managed by the Maine Coastal Islands National Wildlife Refuge.

POND ISLAND LIGHT MOUTH KENNEBEC RIVER ME 64.

11

ROCKLAND BREAKWATER LIGHT, ROCKLAND. In June 1900, Congress appropriated $30,000 for a lighthouse at the outer end of the Rockland breakwater. The station had a one-and-a-half story, gambrel-roofed, wood-frame keeper's dwelling with an attached brick fog signal building. The lantern held a fourth-order Fresnel lens with a focal plane of 30 feet. The keepers' families did not live at the station until 1915. The light was automated in 1965.

WOOD ISLAND LIGHTHOUSE, BIDDEFORD. In 1806, a wooden octagonal tower and a 17-by-26-foot cottage were built on eight acres of land. By 1838, a new rubblestone tower was built to replace the wooden structure. The year 1854 saw the need for further improvement, and a new 47-foot tower and attached one-and-a-half-story dwelling was built; it was again enlarged in 1906 to a full two stories in the Dutch Colonial style. In the late 1960s, the lantern room was removed.

Cape Elizabeth Lighthouse, Cape Elizabeth. In 1828, it was decided to use two lights, a fixed light in the east tower and a revolving light in the west tower, to lessen the confusion with nearby lights. These twin lights were built on 12 acres of land with the towers spaced 895 feet apart. The look of the station changed many times over the years, sometimes from the paint color to how the lights were lit. In 1865, the west tower had one vertical red band, while the east tower had four horizontal red bands. After an attempt at discontinuing the west light in 1883, it was soon relit. By 1924, all twin light stations were to be only single lights, and the west light was shut down permanently. The east light was automated in 1963.

LIGHT HOUSE, MONHEGAN ISLAND, ME. 2.

MONHEGAN LIGHTHOUSE, MONHEGAN. Monhegan Island is 10 miles southwest of Port Clyde on the Maine coast. In the language of the Penobscot Indians, the name means "far away island," as they rowed to the island for fishing. In 1824, on a high hill, the 38-foot-tall stone tower was first lit to help with navigation. There was also a one-and-a-half-story keeper's house measuring 20 by 34 feet. By 1850, the old stone tower was replaced with a 30-foot-tall circular tower made of granite blocks with a second-order Fresnel lens. Additions were made through the years to improve the keeper's living conditions. In 1859, the light was automated with a revolving aerobeacon.

PEMAQUID POINT LIGHTHOUSE, BRISTOL. In 1631, immigrants from Bristol, England, started a settlement at Pemaquid Point, but it was 1826 before a rubblestone tower and a 20-by-34-foot keeper's house made the point important to navigation. Barely eight years later, another tower was needed to replace the original, and this one was 30 feet up to the lantern with a 16-foot diameter base and 10 feet at the top. By 1857, the tower received a fourth-order Fresnel lens, and the need for a new keeper's house was acted upon. This light station was known for its ease of approaching from land, but access from the sea was difficult. In 1934, Pemaquid Point was converted to an automatic acetylene gas operation. In 1940, the residents of Bristol, Maine, purchased the property, with the Coast Guard still maintaining the tower.

OWLS HEAD LIGHTHOUSE, OWLS HEAD. In 1825, a lighthouse was built on 17 acres on the south side of Rockland Harbor after approval from Pres. John Quincy Adams. By 1852, the original stone tower was in need of replacement. A 24-foot-tall round tower was built along with a new one-and-a-half-story keeper's house framed in wood. The tower had a fourth-order Fresnel lens when completed in 1856. In 1903, a covered walkway linking the house to the tower was completed. In 1932, after the tower was electrified, the need for the covered walkway seemed unnecessary, and with the expense of the upkeep, it was removed permanently. Owls Head became automated in 1989, and by 2007, it came under the care of the American Lighthouse Foundation.

SEGUIN ISLAND LIGHTHOUSE, PHIPPSBURG. Seguin Island sits about two-and-a-half miles from the mouth of the Kennebec River and has the distinction of having been authorized by Pres. George Washington. Although the tower is only 53 feet high, the 1857 light is the highest lighthouse above sea level in Maine. Petitions showing the need for a light in the area went as far back as 1786. The original wooden tower was replaced in 1819 with a new stone tower and stone dwelling. In 1856, Congress approved the rebuilding of the light tower and keeper's dwelling, and these improvements can still be seen today. The round tower with its first-order Fresnel lens was built of granite blocks, with the keeper's house constructed with bricks. By 2000, a petition caused the Coast Guard to change its mind about removing the original Fresnel lens.

MARSHALL POINT LIGHTHOUSE, PORT CLYDE. The Marshall Point Light is on a rocky ledge at the end of the St. George Peninsula. The first tower was built in 1832, and both the 20-by-46-foot keeper's dwelling and the tower were built using rubblestone. The two-story dwelling had three rooms on each floor. As with most light towers, the need to replace the original came quickly by 1857, when a 24-foot-tall round tower was built of granite and brick. A fifth-order Fresnel lens with a fixed white light was added at that time. By 1879, the stone keeper's house was renovated with new windows, chimneys, and flooring. In 1895, a Colonial Revival–style home was constructed of wood. The light station was automated in 1971.

Matinicus Rock Lighthouses, Matinicus Rock, Me.

MATINICUS ROCK LIGHTHOUSE, MATINICUS. In 1827, Maine saw the first of two twin-tower lighthouses to be built. It was a necessary place to put a lighthouse, but it was very inhospitable for the keepers to live. The original stone keeper's house had two wooden towers attached to each end of the stone dwelling. By 1846, the need for rebuilding was in progress, and even then, the towers were not spaced the correct amount apart to be useful for navigation. In 1856, two granite towers were constructed with a spacing of 180 feet. Buildings were erected as keepers were added. In 1883, the north light was discontinued, but in 1888 the government reversed the policy, and the north tower was once again in use. By 1923, the north tower was permanently discontinued. In 1983, the remaining light was automated.

Matinicus Rock Light Station, near Matinicus, Me.

BASS HARBOR HEAD LIGHTHOUSE, BASS HARBOR. Mount Desert Island is the largest island on the Maine coast, and the Bass Head Light sits at its southernmost point. In 1858, a light was needed to guide mariners safely into Bass Harbor. The light sits on a granite bluff 56 feet above sea level, giving the 32-foot tower a visibility of 13 miles. The keeper's home was a 20-by-40-foot wooden building that connected to the tower by a wooden walkway. The two-story dwelling had five rooms on the first floor and two on the second. Over the years, modifications were made to update the tower and keeper's dwellings. The light was automated in 1974, and is now in the care of the Coast Guard.

Boon Island, Light off Portsmouth, N. H.

BOON ISLAND LIGHTHOUSE, BOON ISLAND. In 1854, after several previous attempts to light this dangerously small granite isle just over six miles from Maine's coast, a 133-foot-tall granite tower was built. It had 175 steps to reach the top of the tower with its second-order Fresnel lens. Once this tower was built, a second lighthouse keeper was necessary at the site. It is the tallest light tower on the New England coast.

BAKERS ISLAND LIGHTHOUSE, ISLESFORD. On the 123-acre Bakers Island, a rubblestone tower was built in 1828 to a height of 26 feet. With a rough iron frame around its lantern room, it was topped with a copper dome. In 1855, a 45-foot tower and a one-and-a-half-story keeper's dwelling replaced the original. The tower was deactivated in 1955 and reactivated in 1957 as an unattended light.

21

WINTER HARBOR LIGHTHOUSE, WINTER HARBOR. The original service of the Winter Harbor Light Station was from 1857 until 1933, when it directed safe passage into Winter Harbor on Mark Island just one mile from the mainland. The original keeper's house was a one-and-a-half-story wood frame dwelling. A round brick tower 19 feet tall with an octagonal lantern room surrounded by a wrought iron railing, it soon brought light into the harbor with a fifth-order Fresnel lens. By 1876, the dwelling had decayed to the point where a new two-story house was built just north of the original. In 1934, the station was put up for auction and sold to private owners.

INDIAN ISLAND LIGHTHOUSE, ROCKPORT. In 1849, Congress approved a lighthouse at the entrance to Rockport Harbor at Beauchamp Point. It was soon built on the small seven-acre island known then as Indian Island. Both names have been used for this light over the years. The first light was a brick dwelling with the light built on its roof. In 1857, Congress felt a number of the lighthouses in the area should be discontinued, and Indian Island was one of them. By 1874, continuing navigation to the area made restoring this light station imperative. In 1934, the light was once again discontinued and soon sold at auction; the lighthouse and light have been in the same family ever since.

BURNT COAT HARBOR LIGHTHOUSE (HOCKAMOCK HEAD), SWANS ISLAND. At the entrance to Burnt Coat Harbor, a light station was built on the southernmost point called Hockamock Head on Swans Island in 1872. Originally built with twin towers to be used as range lights, the second light was removed in 1884. A story-and-a-half white clapboard keeper's house that connected to the 32-foot tower was erected with a lantern room to house the fourth-order Fresnel lens. In 1975, the original Fresnel lens was removed and replaced with an automatic light nearby, soon found to be not as bright. In 1978, the tower was relit with a 250mm optic lens. Now maintained by the Town of Swans Island, it is listed in the National Register of Historic Places.

HENDRICKS HEAD LIGHTHOUSE, SOUTHPORT. At the mouth of the Sheepscot River, on the western side of Southport Island, a light was erected in 1829. In 1857, a fifth-order Fresnel lens was installed in the tower, giving it better light. In 1875, due to the decay of the original light, a new 40-foot square brick tower was built. A 31-by-22-foot, one-and-a-half-story keeper's cottage was also built. In 1935, after being discontinued, the lighthouse and land were sold to private owners. When electricity came to the island in 1951, the owner allowed the Coast Guard to automate and reinstate the light. A modern light was added when the fifth-order Fresnel lens was removed in 1979. The light remains in private ownership today.

SOUTHPORT, ME.   Hendricks Head Light.   Established 1829.   876

franklin Island Light, Muscongus Bay, Me.

FRANKLIN ISLAND LIGHTHOUSE, FRIENDSHIP. In 1854, a third light was built on Franklin Island at the entrance of the St. George River. The light was a circular brick tower that housed a fourth-order Fresnel lens in the lantern room. A six-room, one-and-a-half-story keeper's house was built with a small storage room that connected the house to the tower. In 1933, the tower was automated. The buildings no longer stand.

Castine, Me.   Dyce's Head Light

DICE HEAD LIGHTHOUSE, CASTINE. In 1828, a 42-foot rubblestone conical tower was built on the Penobscot River in Castine, Maine. The tower was covered in wooden siding in 1857, and a fourth-order Fresnel lens was added at that time. In 1937 the light was automated, and the town took over care of the tower and buildings. In 2007, it was once again lit.

Egg Rock Light, Frenchmans Bay, Maine

EGG ROCK LIGHT, BAR HARBOR. The light on Egg Rock was a 12-foot square tower that rose from the center of a square keeper's dwelling. This light did not use the usual spiral stairs, but rather straight stairs leading up to the lantern room. The tower held a fifth-order Fresnel lens with a fixed red light. It became automated in 1976 and remains an active aid to navigation today.

White Head, Me., White Head Light.

WHITEHEAD LIGHTHOUSE, PENOBSCOT BAY. After a number of previous lights failed when the Lighthouse Board was formed in 1852, the current tower was built using granite blocks. The lantern room held a third-order Fresnel lens and replaced the lamps and reflectors previously used. A stone keeper's dwelling was removed in 1891 and replaced with a framed two-family dwelling. The light was automated in 1982.

TENANTS HARBOR LIGHTHOUSE, ST. GEORGE. The 22-acre Southern Island sits at the entrance to Tenant's Harbor. In 1857, a 27-foot-tall brick tower with an attached wood-frame keeper's house was built. The tower housed a fourth-order Fresnel lens with a 13-mile visibility. A change in 1863 saw a fifth-order lens replace the previous light. The light was discontinued in 1934 and sold to private owners.

GOAT ISLAND LIGHTHOUSE, KENNEBUNKPORT. Goat Island is a three-acre island a mile from Cape Porpoise. In 1831, a conical rubblestone 20-foot-tall tower with an octagon lantern and a wrought-iron railing was built. By 1859, a new cylindrical brick tower standing 25 feet tall was built. Along with a one-and-a-half-story wood-frame keeper's dwelling, a covered walkway attached to the tower was constructed. The light was automated in 1990.

WEST QUODDY HEAD LIGHT, LUBEC.
As marine navigation increased, by 1808, the need for a light at Passamaquoddy Bay was undeniable. By 1831, Congress approved funds for a replacement of this first light. Because the previous lights lacked the ability to adequately light the bay, a conical 48-foot third replacement light was required by 1857. Then a fixed third-order Fresnel lens was placed in the new brick tower. A wood-frame keeper's dwelling was built, and in 1899, the dwelling was made into a duplex for separate living spaces for both keeper's and assistant keeper's families. The daymarks are red and white bands circling the tower. In 1988, West Quoddy Light was automated. The light still operates today and has a visibility of 15 to 18 miles.

QUODDY HEAD LIGHT MOST EASTERN POINT IN U.S.A., LUBEC, ME. 30K,

WEST QUODDY LIGHT — LUBEC, MAINE

- 1913 -

Portland, Me.,
Bug Light Breakwater

PORTLAND BREAKWATER LIGHTHOUSE, SOUTH PORTLAND. In 1936, work began on a breakwater to help guide mariners through the shoal-laced entrance to Portland Harbor. In 1855, an octagonal wooden tower on ashlar stone was completed with a sixth-order Fresnel lens. In 1873, the breakwater was extended an additional 400 feet, and a room was built and connected to the tower on the same foundation. By 1875, the wooden tower had to be replaced with a 26-foot-tall cast-iron tower. In 1889, a handrail was added to the 1,900-foot-long breakwall to make the keeper's journey to the light safer in icy and wet conditions. Portland Breakwater Light was electrified in 1934, and the additional dwelling connected to the tower was removed. The light was discontinued in 1942.

Breakwater Light, Portland, Me.

LIGHTHOUSE, PROSPECT HARBOR, ME. B.W.

PROSPECT HARBOR LIGHTHOUSE, PENOBSCOT BAY. In 1849, the original light and keeper's house were constructed of granite. By 1856, there was no need for the light, and it was discontinued. The decision was reversed within 10 years. By 1891, a 38-foot wooden tower and a newly framed keeper's house were built as replacements. The light was automated in 1934. A fire in 2022 left the keeper's house's fate in doubt.

Mark Island Light, near Stonington, Me.

DEER ISLAND THOROFARE LIGHTHOUSE, PENOBSCOT BAY. In 1857, Congress approved the construction of a square brick tower with a connecting wood-frame keeper's dwelling on the six-acre Mark Island. The tower had a fourth-order Fresnel lens with a visibility of 12 miles. In 1878, the dwelling was whitewashed. A 1958 fire rendered the dwelling a total loss, with only the tower saved.

Maine, Burnt Island Light.

BURNT ISLAND LIGHT STATION, SOUTHPORT. Burnt Island is at the western entrance to the protected waters around Booth Bay Harbor. Burnt Island got its name because the farmers there regularly set fire to the land to improve the grazing for sheep. In 1821, Booth Bay Harbor petitioned Congress for a lighthouse on Burnt Island. A 30-foot-tall, conical granite tower lined with bricks was built. By 1857, a new lantern room was added for the fourth-order Fresnel lens. At the same time, a wood-frame dwelling with a connecting covered walkway replaced the original stone dwelling. The light was automated in 1988.

Burnt Island Light, off Old Orchard, Me.

CUCKOLDS LIGHTHOUSE, SOUTHPORT. Booth Bay Harbor was considered a harbor of refuge for the many ships that entered this bay. But it was not until 1891 that it was approved for a light. A large wood-frame two-story dwelling was built. It was divided into two separate living quarters, with each consisting of a kitchen, a sitting room, two bedrooms, and a bathroom on the second floor. A fog signal building was constructed on a foundation in a semicircle of granite for the pier, making it 36 feet around and 12 feet high. By 1907, a small tower was built on top of the circular roof of the fog building for the fourth-order Fresnel lens. The light station was automated in 1974.

Browns Head Light, Maine.

BROWNS HEAD LIGHTHOUSE, VINALHAVEN. In 1831, the Browns Head Light was built on the northwest corner of Vinalhaven Island to help navigate shipping through the mile-wide straight that runs between the Fox Islands. The octagonal, rubblestone tower stood 22 feet tall and featured a wrought-iron lantern room with a fixed white light. In 1857, a one-and-a-half-story wood-frame dwelling was built, attached to the tower by a covered passageway. The tower was fitted with a fifth-order Fresnel lens. While most lighthouses had the use of assistant light keepers as well as a head keeper, Browns Head was considered a "stag station," where only one keeper was needed. The light was automated in 1987.

BROWNS HEAD LIGHT — VINALHAVEN, MAINE

HALF WAY ROCK LIGHTHOUSE, BAILEY ISLAND. This small island is partway between Cape Elizabeth and Cape Small in the middle of Casco Bay. By 1871, after attempts were made for many years, a 70-foot granite tower, also used as a dwelling for keepers, was constructed. The kitchen was on the first floor, and the keeper lived on the second floor, with any assistant keepers having rooms on the third floor. It was automated in 1975.

HERON NECK LIGHTHOUSE, VINALHAVEN. This lighthouse was constructed in 1853 as a cylindrical brick tower attached to a one-and-a-half-story brick keeper's house. By 1895, the keeper's dwelling was replaced with a wood-frame house. In the early 1900s, a fourth-order Fresnel lens replaced the original fifth-order lens. The light was automated in 1982.

WHALES-BACK LIGHT, PORTSMOUTH HARBOR.
COPYRIGHT, 1904, BY H. PEARSON.

WHALEBACK LEDGE LIGHTHOUSE, KITTERY. A foundation pier was built in 1830 using rough-split granite blocks, 48 feet in diameter at the base and 22 feet high. A stone conical tower 32 feet high was built on the foundation. In 1869, the new tower was built of large granite blocks dovetailed together and bolted to the ledge. This new tower site was covered with water except at low tide. The fourth-order lens was transferred from the old tower into the new one. In 1881, a covered walkway was built to connect the tower to the fog signal building. In 1963, the light was automated.

Portsmouth, N.H.,
Whaleback Light,
Portsmouth Harbor.

Two

NEW HAMPSHIRE

1771 PORTSMOUTH HARBOR LIGHTHOUSE (FORT POINT), NEW CASTLE. Royal governor John Wentworth had a hexagonal wooden lighthouse built at Fort Point in Portsmouth Harbor in 1771. It was one of 11 lighthouses in the 13 colonies established before the American Revolution.

Fort Constitution, New Castle, N. H.

PORTSMOUTH HARBOR LIGHTHOUSE (FORT POINT), NEW CASTLE. Fort William and Mary, so named by the British, was rebuilt after the Revolution and named Fort Constitution in 1800. A new light was built in 1804 a short distance from the original, and a wooden bridge was used to access the light. The tower was 80 feet tall, with the keeper residing in the village, not at the light. By 1851, the tower was shortened to 55 feet, and a fourth-order Fresnel lens was added. The lighthouse was replaced in 1877 with a cast-iron tower lined with brick. A brown color was used as its daymark. In 1902, the color changed to white. The light was automated in 1960 and came under the care of the Friends of Portsmouth Harbor Lighthouses in 2001.

Fort Point Light, New Castle, N. H.

SURF, WHITE ISLAND LIGHT, ISLES OF SHOALS, N.H.

ISLE OF SHOALS LIGHTHOUSE (WHITE ISLAND), RYE. Nine islands make up the Isle of Shoals, just six miles off the coasts of Maine and New Hampshire. The 40-foot-tall first light tower and house were built of rubblestone in 1820. Because of the intensity of the storms, the covered walkway was washed away a number of times. In 1859, a replacement tower was built of brick, with a second-order Fresnel lens that offered visibility of 15 miles. At the same time, an assistant keeper was added to the light station. In 1877, the original stone keeper's dwelling was replaced and later used for storage, and a wood-frame one-and-a-half-story duplex dwelling was added. The early 1950s saw the removal of the duplex built in 1878, and the dwelling replaced with a more modern residence. The light was automated in 1986.

6030. WHITE ISLAND LIGHT, ISLES OF SHOALS, N.H.

Burke Haven Light, Lake Sunapee, N. H.

LAKE SUNAPEE LIGHTHOUSES, SUNAPEE. From top to bottom, Burke Haven, Herrick Cove, and Loon Lake are three lighthouses on Lake Sunapee. From the 1880s through the 1930s, the lake saw steamers carrying passengers, luggage, and mail to the area's hotels and residences. The Woodsum brothers owned the largest steamer company on the lake and built the Loon Lake light in 1892; soon, the Herrick Cove and Burke Haven lights were added to help with lake traffic. After the steamer traffic ended, the lights were left unattended. Over the years, they suffered numerous hardships until maintenance was taken on by the Lake Sunapee Protective Association. (Herrick Cove postcard courtesy of Jeremy D'Entremont.)

Three

MASSACHUSETTS

Chatham Lights, Chatham, Mass.

CHATHAM LIGHTHOUSE, CHATHAM. Chatham is a Cape Cod town surrounded on three sides by water. On the west lies the Atlantic, while on the south is Nantucket Sound, with Pleasant Bay on the north. The waters around Chatham have very strong currents and dangerous shoals. When this light was built, it was given two lights to distinguish it from the neighboring Highland light.

CHATHAM LIGHTHOUSE, CHATHAM. In 1808, two 40-foot-tall octagonal wooden towers were erected 70 feet apart along with a one-story, three-room keeper's house. By 1841, both towers were torn down and replaced by brick towers also 70 feet apart, along with a new keeper's dwelling 17 by 26 feet in size. The towers were connected to the dwelling with a covered walkway. Due to erosion, a new light station was built across the road in 1877, along with a keeper's dwelling that also included room for an assistant. The south tower received a fourth-order Fresnel lens, and the north tower was removed; it became known as the Nauset Light. The Chatham Light was automated in 1982.

GAY HEAD LIGHTHOUSE, AQUINNAH. Gay Head Light sits on the cliffs of the western end of Martha's Vineyard. The original light was an octagonal wooden tower with a wooden keeper's dwelling. The tower was moved away from the cliffs because of erosion in 1844. By 1854, construction was started on a new 51-foot brick tower and dwelling. In 1899, the house was found to be damp and unsanitary, and a gambrel-roofed, duplex dwelling was built in 1902. The light was electrified in 1952, and its first-order Fresnel lens was removed. With full automation in 1954, the surrounding buildings and house were demolished, and now the redbrick tower sits alone on the cliffs. In 2015, the tower was moved farther away from the cliffs by 175 feet and is now in the care of the Town of Aquinnah.

GAY HEAD LIGHT, MARTHA'S VINEYARD ISLAND, MASS.   804

SANKATY HEAD LIGHTHOUSE, NANTUCKET. In 1849, on the southernmost headland in New England on 10 acres at Sankaty Head, a brick tower 53 feet tall with a nine-foot lantern helped with navigation through the dangerous shoals near Nantucket. A keeper's dwelling was built near the tower for a keeper and two assistants. By 1855, Sankaty Light had only one assistant keeper, and a separate dwelling was built. In 1887, the station's two separate dwellings were replaced with a larger wood-frame duplex. In 1933, electricity came to the light station, making it unnecessary for the assistant keeper. The lighthouse was automated in 1965, and by that time, the Coast Guard had already taken over responsibility for the light. By the mid-1990s, all the surrounding buildings had been removed and only the tower remained.

Sankaty Light
Nantucket, Mass.

BRANT POINT LIGHTHOUSE, NANTUCKET. Before the United States had won its independence from Great Britain, there was a need for a light on the south side near the entrance to Nantucket Harbor. By 1856, after numerous other light towers had failed, a circular brick tower and an attached keeper's dwelling were constructed. The conical tower was built using brick and sandstone. The cast-iron lantern had 12 glass windows. An iron staircase was used to reach the lantern room, which held the fourth-order Fresnel lens. With its elevation of only 26 feet, it is the shortest of the New England lighthouses. Brant Point Light was automated in 1965.

Marblehead Neck Lighthouse, Marblehead, Mass.

MARBLEHEAD LIGHTHOUSE, MARBLEHEAD NECK. In 1835, a light was built on Marblehead Neck in Essex County. It had a 23-foot white brick tower with an octagonal lantern room and a keeper's dwelling attached to the tower by a covered walkway. By 1857, a sixth-order Fresnel lens replaced the oil lamps. The keeper's house was replaced by a larger two-story wood-frame dwelling in 1878. By 1895, a taller tower was needed for the area, and a 100-foot-tall, pyramidal, iron-skeleton tower was constructed. With an iron cylinder inside the tower, it took 127 steps to reach the landing below the lantern room. Support for the tower came from a network of braces attached to cast-iron pilings on the foundation. A covered walkway was attached from the dwelling to the tower. The light was automated in 1960, but the tower still remains the original metallic brown color.

Marblehead Light, Marblehead, Mass.

A 7155   Eastern Point Light House, Cape Ann, Mass.

EASTERN POINT LIGHTHOUSE, GLOUCESTER. On the eastern tip of Gloucester Harbor, the original tower was 30 feet tall. When this light proved inadequate by 1848, it was torn down and a 34-foot brick tower was built. The year 1857 saw a fourth-order Fresnel lens added to the lantern room. A Gothic Revival wooden two-story keeper's dwelling was built in 1879. In 1890, the 1848 brick tower was demolished, and a new 36-foot cylindrical tower was built on the old foundation. During this time, the covered walkway was removed. Electricity came to the station in 1896. The lighthouse was automated in 1985. The public is unable to access the light and grounds, as the Coast Guard is still stationed at the light today.

EASTERN POINT LIGHT, GLOUCESTER, MASS.   1247

NAUSET LIGHT, EASTHAM, CAPE COD, MASS.   5348-29

NAUSET LIGHTHOUSE, EASTHAM. A light was needed midway between the Highland Light and the twin Chatham Lights in 1837. Three lights, called "the Three Sisters," were built along the cliffs, 15 feet tall and 150 feet apart. By 1911, erosion of the cliffs doomed two of the towers. The middle tower was saved, and one of the cast-iron, 48-foot Chatham Lights was discontinued and relocated to Nauset Beach. The light was automated in 1955.

Old Light, Brant Point Nantucket, Mass.

OLD BRANT POINT LIGHTHOUSE, NANTUCKET. A new light at the Nantucket Harbor entrance was constructed in 1856 with a circular brick and sandstone tower with an attached keeper's dwelling. The cast-iron lantern room held a fourth–order Fresnel lens. From 1746, Brant Point saw a total of nine lighthouses until it was automated in 1965.

HOSPITAL POINT FRONT RANGE LIGHTHOUSE, SUDBURY. A light station was established to complete the lighting of Salem Harbor at Hospital Point to help marine navigation into Salem Sound in 1870; in 1872, a 40-foot square white tower with a black lantern room was constructed with a three-and-a-half-order Fresnel lens. A Queen Anne Revival keeper's home was built near the tower. The light was automated in 1947. The name "Hospital Point" comes from a smallpox hospital that was built on the point in 1901 and burned down in 1849. The Coast Guard owns and is responsible for the Hospital Point Lighthouse.

Bass River, Light House, West Dennis, Mass.

BASS RIVER LIGHTHOUSE, WEST DENNIS. In 1853, Congress appropriated funds for a light east of the Bass River. A white, one-and-a-half-story, wood-frame Cape Cod–style keeper's house was constructed with an iron lantern room on the roof. The light was thought unnecessary by 1880, but within a year, it was reactivated. It continued in navigational service until 1914. The light was sold at auction to a private owner, and the main house was enlarged and additional buildings were added. By 1939, the property became the Lighthouse Inn. Although still privately owned, the Bass River Light was relit in August 1989 by the Coast Guard.

THE LIGHTHOUSE, WEST DENNIS BEACH, CAPE COD, MASSACHUSETTS.

CAPE COD LIGHTHOUSE (HIGHLAND), NORTH TRURO. Congress appropriated $8,000, and George Washington approved the construction of this lighthouse in 1796. It was thought that the light should be built on the highlands of Truro, which were 150 feet up from the beach, to help with visibility of the light. By 1856, construction began on a new 60-foot tower that would house a first-order Fresnel lens; in addition, a home for the head keepers and a separate dwelling for the new assistants were added. While many changes took place over the years, the largest concern was erosion. The tower originally stood 510 feet from the cliff edge in 1806. By 1989, it was only 128 feet. The light was automated in 1986.

Lighthouse cuttyhunk mass

CUTTYHUNK LIGHTHOUSE, CUTTYHUNK. Cuttyhunk Island is the farthest island in the Elizabeth Island chain. In 1823, the original 25-foot conical stone tower and single-family home were constructed. The tower was soon encased in brick for strength. In 1857, a fifth-order Fresnel lens was installed. In 1860, a second story was added to the keeper's dwelling with the addition of a square tower and lantern room. The original dwelling was replaced in 1891 with a wood-frame keeper's home. A conical wooden tower was built and attached to the home with a covered walkway. This "temporary" tower lasted half a century. In 1947, the tower and dwelling were removed and a metal skeletal tower was built to hold the light until it was discontinued in 2005.

Lighthouse - Cuttyhunk, Mass.

HYANNIS LIGHTHOUSE, HYANNIS. A section of land was obtained for a small tower with the approval of Congress in 1848 after the fishing industry had grown to great importance in this part of Cape Cod. By 1850, a keeper's dwelling and covered walkway leading to the tower were constructed, and a fifth-order Fresnel lens was fitted into the lantern room a few years later. By 1863, a new cast-iron lantern room was placed on top of the 19-foot conical brick tower. In 1929, the light was decommissioned and the lantern room was removed, and the lighthouse was sold to private owners.

Newburyport, Mass. Plum Island Light.

NEWBURYPORT HARBOR LIGHTHOUSE (PLUM ISLAND), NEWBURYPORT. In 1787, the Massachusetts Assembly approved the construction of two lighthouses with fixed white lights on the north end of Plum Island, the nine-mile-long island that runs along the Massachusetts coast. It was also known as the Plum Island Light. A keeper's dwelling was constructed around the same time as the lights. In 1808, both lights blew over, prompting the need to replace them, but repairs were made instead. In 1856, the front range tower was struck by lightning and burned to the ground. A "bug light," a smaller light, was used to form a range light with the old tower. In 1951, the light was automated.

Plum Island Light and General Store of A. C Ingalls Plum Island, Newburyport, Mass.

CAPE ANN LIGHTHOUSE (THATCHER ISLAND), ROCKPORT. As early as 1771, the need for a lighthouse on Thatcher Island, off Cape Ann near Rockport, was apparent. The two lights were there to make mariners aware of a partly submerged reef near the island. The lights were octagonal, 45 feet tall, and constructed out of wood and stone. Because of how the lights were lined up, the villagers on the mainland named the twin lights "Ann's Eyes." By 1861, two new 124-foot granite towers were constructed to replace the previous lights. First-order Fresnel lenses were placed in the towers, with a 22-mile visibility. With 900 feet between the towers, a head keeper and four assistants were needed. In 1932, the north tower was discontinued. The south tower is operated by the Coast Guard.

THATCHER'S ISLAND, ROCKPORT, MASS.   THE NORTHERN LIGHTHOUSE.

55

MINOT LEDGE LIGHT, BOSTON HARBOR

MINOT'S LEDGE LIGHTHOUSE, BETWEEN COHASSET AND SCITUATE. After a disastrous first attempt and loss of life, by 1855, construction was started on a new light on Outer Minot's Rock, with granite stones weighing two tons each cut on the mainland and transported to the ledge. Work could only be done at low tide for the safety of the workers, and continued until 1860, when a bronze lantern was added to the 100-foot-tall tower. The light was to have a head keeper and three assistant keepers with accommodations in two duplex dwellings in Cohasset for their families. In 1894, a second-order Fresnel lens was installed in the tower. In 1947, the ledge light was electrified and automated, and there was no longer a need for keepers. The light was sold in 2014.

Light House, Scituate, Mass.

Many thanks for cards and nice note. Am having a fine time here — am sorry I can't... a very pretty coast. Regards to all. Edith!

SCITUATE LIGHTHOUSE, BOSTON. In 1810, on the south shore of Boston, a small group of men constructed a 25-foot-tall octagonal granite tower along with a one-and-a-half-story dwelling. By 1827, an additional 15 feet were added to the height of the tower, along with a new lantern to help with visibility. Being close to the powerful Minot's Ledge Light, by 1860, the Scituate Light was discontinued. The Fresnel lens and lantern room were removed, and the property was put up for lease. In 1916, the residents of Scituate bought the light from the government and refurbishing began. The tower was relit in 1994 after being dark for 134 years.

SANDY NECK LIGHTHOUSE, YARMOUTHPORT, MASS.

SANDY NECK LIGHTHOUSE, WEST BARNSTABLE. On a six-mile-long peninsula on the north side of Cape Cod at the entrance to Barnstable Harbor sits a lighthouse constructed in 1826. The original light was a wooden tower 16 feet tall, rising from the center of the keeper's dwelling. It was decided that the tower and dwelling should be separate for safety's sake. In 1857, a 48-foot circular brick tower was built a short distance from the dwelling. In 1880, the keeper's home was replaced with a wood-frame building. In 1887, iron hoops and staves were placed around the tower for additional support and strength. By 1931, the light was decommissioned, and the lantern room and light were removed. The light was sold to private owners in 1933.

Sandy Neck Light.

WOOD END LIGHT AND COAST GUARD STATION, PROVINCETOWN, MASS.

WOOD END LIGHTHOUSE, PROVINCETOWN. In 1872, near Provincetown Harbor, a square, pyramidal brick-built tower was constructed and painted brown with a lantern room and railing painted black. A one-and-a-half-story wood-frame keeper's dwelling was also built a short distance from the tower. By 1896, a new one-and-a-half-story wooden keeper's house was built to replace the original. A stone breakwater was built across the upper end of the harbor in 1911 allowing crossing from Provincetown to the light at low tide, making trips into town easier for the keepers and their families. In 1961, the light was automated, and with no need for a keeper, the house and other buildings were soon torn down.

Wood End Light, Provincetown, Mass.

CLARKS POINT LIGHTHOUSE, NEW BEDFORD. In 1804, a 38-foot-tall stone lighthouse was constructed at the entrance to New Bedford Harbor. It was not until 1842 that a keeper's house was built. By 1857, the government felt a military presence was needed in the area, and a granite fort was constructed. Meanwhile, a new lantern room with larger panes of glass housed a fifth-order Fresnel lens; it had previously been installed in 1856 at the Clarks Point Light. In 1869, the lantern room and keeper's quarters were relocated to the top of Fort Tabor using a new rectangular tower. After the seven-sided fort grew in size, it blocked the light from the lighthouse. The original 1804 tower was torn down in 1906. When it was realized that the need for the fort had passed, construction stopped in 1871.

FORT AT CLARK'S POINT AND OLD LIGHTHOUSE

H. S. HUTCHINSON & CO.   NEW BEDFORD, MASS.

Baker's Island Lights, Beverly, Mass.

BAKER ISLAND LIGHTHOUSE, ISLESFORD. A light was built on Baker Island in 1828 of rubblestone, 26 feet tall with an octagonal lantern. Baker Island was the farthest of the five Cranberry Isles, located at the entrance to Southwest Harbor. In 1855, with the deterioration of the original house and tower, a new one-and-a-half-story keeper's dwelling and a connecting 45-foot-tall brick tower were built. A kitchen wing was added in 1868. The tower was reinforced in 1903 with an external four-inch-thick brick wall. The Baker Island Light was deactivated in late 1955 and reactivated in 1957 to aid navigation, but without a keeper. The National Park Service took over care for the light in 2011.

Copyright 1905 by the Rotograph Co.

G 7210 Twin Lighthouses, Baker's Island, Mass.

Bishop's & Clerks Light, off Hyannis, Mass.

BISHOP AND CLERKS LIGHTHOUSE, HYANNIS. Bishop and Clerks was the most dangerous shoal in Hyannis Harbor, necessitating a light on the shoal. In 1858, a light grey granite 65-foot tower with a wooden attachment for holding the fog bell system was built. The lantern room held a fourth-order Fresnel lens. The light was automated in 1923 and deactivated in 1928. In 1952, the granite tower was demolished in favor of a beacon.

GRAVES LIGHTHOUSE, HULL. In 1903, work started on a 113-foot conical granite light tower on Graves Ledge. The area around the entrance was used for storage, with the engine room one floor above. The kitchen and dining room were on the third level, and the fourth and fifth levels had a library and bunkrooms that could accommodate at least four men. The last two levels held the lantern room, watch room, and Fresnel lens. The light was automated in 1976.

A 7015b The New Graves Light, Boston, Mass.

A 7151   Annisquam Light, Cape Ann, Mass.

ANNISQUAM HARBOR LIGHTHOUSE, GLOUCESTER. This lighthouse was on the north end of the Annisquam River, where a second light tower was constructed in 1851, and then the white octagonal 40-foot tower was built along with repairs to the original keeper's house. Soon, a fifth-order Fresnel lens was in place. In 1867, a 109-foot covered walkway connected the tower and the dwelling. In 1897, the present brick tower was constructed on the same foundation as the original wooden one. A fourth-order Fresnel lens installed in 1922. By 1944, the covering on the walkway was removed. In 1974, the light was fully automated.

ANNISQUAM LIGHT, GLOUCESTER, MASS.   18

BIRD ISLAND LIGHTHOUSE, MARION. On the south coast of Massachusetts sits Sippican Harbor. In 1819, a 29-foot rubblestone tower with a covered walkway connecting to a stone dwelling was constructed. In 1890, the old stone dwelling was replaced with a wood-frame house on the original foundation. In 1940, the light was put up for auction, and the Town of Marion owns it today.

FORT PICKERING (WINTER ISLAND) LIGHTHOUSE, SALEM. At the entrance to Salem Harbor, in 1870, a cast-iron brick-lined tower with a fifth-order Fresnel lens was constructed offshore and attached to the island by a wooden walkway 52 feet long. This walkway required rebuilding twice over the years. The tower was usually painted brown or red as its daymark. When the Coast Guard left the island in 1970, the light was abandoned.

Ipswich Light, Ipswich, Mass.

3911-PUB. BY I. E. B. PERK.NS. IPSWICH MASS.

IPSWICH RANGE LIGHTHOUSE, GLOUCESTER. In 1837, twin lights, 29 feet tall with an inner layer of brick and an outer layer of cement, were constructed here. The towers were 542 feet apart. A one-and-a-half-story keeper's dwelling was built of brick and had a shingled roof. By 1932, the front range light was discontinued, and the rear light was automated.

Ned Point Light, Mattapoisett, Mass.

NED'S POINT LIGHT, MATTAPOISETT. Ned's Point on Buzzards Bay is near the town of Mattapoisett, where in 1837, beach rubble was used to build a 35-foot stone tower with a cast-iron "bird cage" lantern room. By 1956, a fifth-order Fresnel lens replaced the original lamps. In 1939, the light was put up for auction and is now in private ownership.

4409
WING NECK LIGHT HOUSE, POCASSET, CAPE COD, MASS.

WINGS NECK LIGHTHOUSE, POCASSET. The original 1849 Cape Cod–style keeper's dwelling had an attached wooded hexagonal tower. Between 1889 and 1899, after tearing down the original dwelling, a new wood-frame keeper's home was built on the same foundation, and a covered walkway connected to the new hexagonal tower. By 1923, the light was automated.

SOUVENIR POST CARD CO. N.Y.   5906—Palmers Island Light House, New Bedford, Mass

PALMER ISLAND LIGHTHOUSE, NEW BEDFORD. In 1849, a conical, 24-foot-tall rubblestone tower with a birdcage-style lantern room was installed on the northernmost point of the island. The keeper's dwelling was on a higher point of land, and connected to the tower by a walkway. To help protect the tower, a 99-foot seawall was built. In 1856, a fifth-order Fresnel lens was added. The light was no longer used by 1963.

NOBSKA POINT LIGHTHOUSE, FALMOUTH. The original light built in 1828 was a one-and-a-half-story Cape Cod–style dwelling with an octagonal tower on top of the keeper's house. Stress due to the weight of the lantern room made changing the tower necessary. In 1876, a 40-foot cast-iron brick-lined tower was built along with a wood-frame dwelling. A covered walkway was also added in 1899. The fifth-order lens was used until 1887, when a fourth-order lens replaced it. The light was automated in 1985 and became home to the Coast Guard Auxiliary.

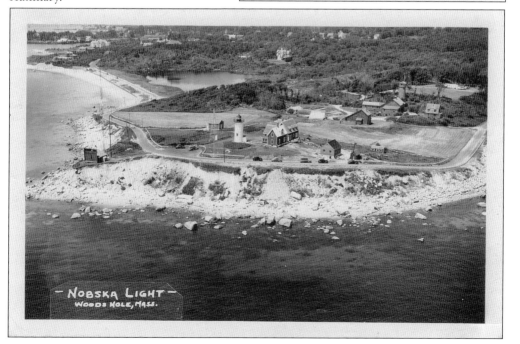

— NOBSKA LIGHT —
WOODS HOLE, MASS.

EDGARTOWN HARBOR LIGHTHOUSE, EDGARTOWN. In 1828, the first lighthouse here was a two-story dwelling with a lantern room centered on the roof. A 1,500-foot walkway was built to connect the dwelling to the mainland. A stone pier soon replaced the original wood base of the light. In 1938, a hurricane caused extensive damage to the light. From 1939 through 1980, the light was maintained by the Coast Guard, which refurbished the dwelling in 1985. By 2014, the Town of Edgartown took ownership of the lighthouse.

Four

RHODE ISLAND

SOUTH EAST LIGHTHOUSE, BLOCK ISLAND, R. I.

BLOCK ISLAND SOUTH EAST LIGHTHOUSE, NORTH SHOREHAM, 1874. Block Island is south of the Rhode Island coast and lies in the middle of the east-west and north-south shipping lanes. In 1872, Congress appropriated $75,000 to build a lighthouse on the south coast of the island. It was always going to be a special light, so a brick dwelling with an attached 67-foot tower with a first-order lens were designed in High Victorian Gothic style with Italianate influences.

South East Light House, Block Island, R. I.

BLOCK ISLAND SOUTH EAST LIGHTHOUSE, NORTH SHOREHAM. The redbrick 52-foot tower was constructed in 1874 on the Mohegan Bluffs on the south end of Block Island. The cast-iron lantern was 15 feet tall and held a fixed first-order Fresnel lens. The keeper's dwelling was attached to the tower, where the keeper had one side and the assistant keeper had rooms on the other side. When the light was built, it was 300 feet to the cliff edge; by the early 1990s, it was only 55 feet, and the light was relocated a safe distance by the International Chimney Company. This company went on to relocate a number of other lighthouses in peril. After the move, the light received a first-order Fresnel lens that had been used in the Cape Lookout Lighthouse in North Carolina and which still aids in the navigation of the area today.

SOUTH LIGHT & FOG HORNS, BLOCK ISLAND, R. I.

BRISTOL FERRY LIGHT HOUSE, BRISTOL, R. I.

BRISTOL FERRY LIGHTHOUSE, BRISTOL. Under the Mount Hope Bridge, which crosses over the passage between Narragansett Bay and Mount Hope Bay, sits the Bristol Ferry Lighthouse. In 1854, a brick two-story keeper's house with living quarters on both floors was built with an attached 28-foot-tall tower with a sixth-order Fresnel lens. By 1902, a new cast-iron lantern room replaced the previous wooden one, and a fifth-order lens was added. In 1927, the light was retired at the same time the Mount Hope Bridge was being built. It was then sold into private ownership a number of times and remains a private structure today.

Bristol Ferry Light, NARRAGANSETT BAY, R. I.   10586

A 6863   Point Judith Light, Narragansett Pier, R. J.

many days the same, Mary.

POINT JUDITH LIGHTHOUSE, NARRAGANSETT. Point Judith is on the western side of the entrance to Narragansett Bay. In 1857, an octagonal brownstone tower 65 feet tall was built along with a brick keeper's dwelling attached to the tower. A fourth-order Fresnel lens in the lantern room had a visibility of 16 miles out to sea. In 1899, the top half of the tower was painted brown, keeping the lower half white for its daymark. In 1938, New England was hit by a major hurricane, and in Point Judith, the cliffs surrounding the light lost as much as 250 feet of the sea wall. In 1954, the light station was automated and the keeper's dwelling demolished. In 2013, Point Judith was one of the lighthouses featured by the US Postal Service on its lighthouse stamps.

Narragansett Pier, R.I., Point Judith Light.

BEAVERTAIL LIGHTHOUSE, JAMESTOWN. The fourth tower to be built here, the Beavertail Light was a 58-foot brick and stone tower constructed in 1754. In 1856, a granite block, 52-foot tower replaced the worn-out previous tower. A third-order Fresnel lens was placed in the 10-foot lantern room with a fixed white light. At the same time, a two-story brick keeper's dwelling was constructed, and when completed, the previous light tower and dwelling were demolished. In 1899, the Fresnel lens was downgraded to a fourth-order lens, and the upper half of the unpainted granite tower was painted white. Beavertail Light was automated in 1972. The light station is still an active aid to navigation in the area.

NORTH LIGHT HOUSE, BLOCK ISLAND, R.I.

BLOCK ISLAND NORTH LIGHTHOUSE, NEW SHOREHAM. There were at least four lighthouses built over the years on the north end of the six-mile-long Block Island. The year 1837 saw a rectangular granite keeper's dwelling with a light tower at each end of the roof. These two lights were lined up north-south and looked like one light until ships were within two or three miles of the lighthouse. In 1867, the current lighthouse was built in the Victorian and Gothic Revival style as a two-story dwelling with Connecticut granite. The pitched slate-covered roof had an iron lantern room and tower on the northern end. Block Island Lighthouse was automated in 1956, and by 1973, it had been deactivated.

North Light House, Block Island, R.I.

MUSSELBED SHOALS LIGHTHOUSE, BRISTOL POINT. In 1873, on the Musselbed Shoal, a square house was constructed for use of the light keepers, and a lantern room for the light was placed on the roof. This structure sat on a stone and block pier. In 1924, the original light was demolished and replaced with a larger four-room dwelling. Because of ice and inclement weather, this structure was rebuilt numerous times, and in 1938, it was demolished for good.

Breakwater Light, Newport, R. I.

NEWPORT HARBOR LIGHTHOUSE, NEWPORT. By 1842, a second tower, 35 feet tall and granite, was constructed on this small island along with a breakwater over the reef extending out from the island to the light. By 1855, the light tower had a fifth-order-Fresnel lens. In 1864, a keeper's house was constructed at the end of the breakwater. The lighthouse was automated in 1963 and sold to a private developer.

Warwick Neck Light.   Warwick, R. I.

WARWICK NECK LIGHTHOUSE, WARWICK. In 1826, a 30-foot stone tower and attached small stone keeper's dwelling were built here. The lantern room had a fourth-order Fresnel lens added in 1856. By 1889, a one-and-a-half-story wood-frame house was built, and the original addition became a barn. In 1932, a new tower was needed because of erosion, and a 31-foot steel tower was constructed. In 1985, the lighthouse was automated.

Warwick Neck Light House,
Rocky Point, R. I.

261

Sakonnet Lighthouse, Little Compton. In 1884, a light was placed on the concrete-filled foundation. A cylindrical, cast-iron tower with a lantern room and watch room with four more floors were used as living quarters. The light endured storms and rough seas for much of the year, necessitating constant repairs. After the 1954 hurricane, due to repair costs, the light was deactivated.

Conimicut Lighthouse. Warwick. Built in 1883, this spark plug–style 58-foot cast-iron caisson lighthouse was built to replace a previous 1868 light. In 1960, the Conimicut Light was the last lighthouse to convert from oil to electricity, and shortly after that, The light was automated. The City of Warwick took on responsibility for the light and continues to refurbish and care for the light.

SAKONNET LIGHTHOUSE, SAKONNET, R. I.

Conimicut Light, NARRAGANSETT BAY, R. I.   10587

ROSE ISLAND LIGHTHOUSE, NEWPORT. In 1869, a lighthouse was built on Rose Island because of its importance to marine traffic coming into Newport Harbor. The wood-frame two-story lighthouse has a mansard roof where the short octagonal tower and lantern room with a sixth-order Fresnel lens sit atop the dwelling. After the Newport Bridge was opened in 1969, the light became obsolete. The Rose Island Light was deactivated in 1971.

SABIN POINT LIGHT, PROVIDENCE RIVER. A Second Empire–style two-story granite lighthouse was constructed in 1872 on the east side of the Providence River. The lighthouse managed to survive the hurricane of 1938. By 1956, it was automated. Due to widening of the shipping channel in the river in 1968, the light was burned down and removed.

Watch Hill Light, Watch Hill, R. I.

WATCH HILL LIGHTHOUSE, WATCH HILL. After erosion brought the edge of the bluff too close, a previous lighthouse here was demolished, and in 1856, a new light was built on Watch Hill at the eastern entrance to Fishers Island Sound. The 10-foot square tower with a height of 45 feet was constructed using 10-inch-thick granite blocks and attached to the southeast corner of the two-story keeper's dwelling. The lantern room held a fourth-order Fresnel lens. The dwelling had room for a kitchen, dining room, living area, and three bedrooms. The light was automated in 1986 and a modern beacon replaced the Fresnel lens. The National Historical Lighthouse Preservation Act has helped maintain the lighthouse and has kept it free from vandalism.

WATCH HILL, R. I.   LIGHT-HOUSE POINT.

Dutch Island Light.   Narragansett Bay, R. I.

DUTCH ISLAND, JAMESTOWN. A second lighthouse was built near Conanicut Island in Narragansett Bay on a small outcrop called Dutch Island in 1856. A 42-foot square brick tower with a fourth-order Fresnel lens was attached to the two-story brick keeper's dwelling. The light was automated in 1947 and deactivated in 1972, as it had outlived its usefulness.

Gould's Island Light.   Narragansett Bay, R. I.

GOULD ISLAND LIGHTHOUSE, NARRAGANSETT BAY. A lighthouse was established on Gould Island in Narragansett Bay in 1889. A 30-foot brick lighthouse with a fifth-order Fresnel lens was built, along with a keeper's dwelling a short distance from the tower. By 1947, the light was discontinued and replaced with a skeletal tower and new automated light. The 1889 tower was torn down in 1960.

IDA LEWIS ROCK LIGHTHOUSE, NEW PORT HARBOR. On Lime Rock at the southern end of New Port Harbor, a brick tower with a sixth-order Fresnel lens and an attached two-story Greek Revival–style granite dwelling was built in 1856. The first keeper was Hosea Lewis. After an intense illness, his 16-year-old daughter Ida took over the work involved at the light. As was the custom, with her father's death in 1872, her mother was appointed keeper until she retired in 1879 and Ida was given the position. She remained the keeper until her death in 1911. Deactivated in 1927, the light was sold at auction to become a yacht club. The Lime Rock Lighthouse had been renamed the Ida Lewis Rock Lighthouse because of Ida's accomplishments.

Pomham Light. Providence, R. I.

POMHAM ROCKS LIGHTHOUSE, RIVERSIDE. In 1870, the Pomham Rocks Lighthouse was built on this rocky outcropping in the Providence River. The Victorian-style square two-story, seven-room dwelling had a 40-foot tower attached to the mansard roof. A sixth-order Fresnel lens was fitted in the lantern room. The lens was exchanged for a fourth-order lens in 1939. In 1974, the light was deactivated and put up for auction.

Bullock Point Light, near Providence, R. I.

BULLOCK POINT LIGHTHOUSE, RIVERSIDE. In 1875, after enlarging the pier over the Bullock Point Shoal in the Providence River, a keeper's dwelling, light tower, and lantern on top of the roof were built. In 1938, a hurricane came through the area, and the Bullock Point Lighthouse was damaged beyond any hope of repair. By 1939, the light was discontinued, and the dwelling and tower were torn down shortly after.

Five

CONNECTICUT

Bridgeport Light, Bridgeport, Conn

BRIDGEPORT HARBOR LIGHTHOUSE, BRIDGEPORT. A second lighthouse with a stone break wall around the dwelling was built in 1871 on the west side of Bridgeport Harbor. The light was a square dwelling with a mansard roof and a white tower for the lantern room that housed a fourth-order Fresnel lens. By 1953 the lighthouse was redundant, and while in the process of dismantling the light, an accidental fire destroyed the lighthouse.

Smith Island Light, Norwalk Harbor, Conn.

SHEFFIELD ISLAND LIGHTHOUSE, NORWALK HARBOR. "Smith Island Light" is one of many names this light had through the years. There are 16 islands in the Norwalk Island chain, and Sheffield is the largest. In 1869, a new schoolhouse-style keeper's dwelling with two and a half stories was erected out of granite stone. The tower was 46 feet tall and was fitted with a fourth-order Fresnel lens. The old light tower was torn down, and the previous keeper's house was used as a storage building. The light was deactivated in 1902 and sold at auction in 1914.

SMITH ISLAND LIGHT, SO. NORWALK, CONN.

THE STRATFORD LIGHT HOUSE, STRATFORD, CONN.

STRATFORD POINT LIGHTHOUSE, STRATFORD. In 1880, at the entrance to the Housatonic River, a new two-story keeper's dwelling with eight rooms was built to replace the original 1821 light. A new 40-foot-tall cast-iron tower was constructed on a concrete foundation with an inner brick lining. The white-painted tower housed a third-order Fresnel lens. By 1899, the daymark on the tower was changed, giving it a reddish-brown large band around the tower. In 1906, a fourth-order lens replaced the third-order lens. The light was automated in 1969, and the lantern room was removed from the tower. In 1990, after a refurbishing of the lantern room, it was returned to the tower after the installation of a smaller optic lamp. The light still helps with navigation today.

Stratford Point Light House, Stratford, Conn.

Latimer Reef Light, Stonington, Conn.

LATIMER REEF LIGHTHOUSE, FISHER ISLAND SOUND. In 1884, a "spark plug" or "coffee pot" style white cylindrical 49-foot cast-iron tower was constructed with a concrete-filled, cast-iron foundation on the reef just north of Fishers Island Sound. In 1899, a fourth-order Fresnel lens replaced the original fifth-order lens. The white-painted tower also received a brownish-red band around the middle. The light was automated in 1954.

Breakwater Light House, New Haven, Conn.

THE SOUTHWEST LEDGE LIGHTHOUSE, NEW HAVEN. This light was at the entrance to the shipping channel in New Haven Harbor. The 45-foot-tall tower was constructed with a distinctive eight-sided, three-story cast-iron dwelling with a mansard roof. It was placed on a caisson foundation that was strengthened with concrete. The first two stories were living quarters for the keepers, with the remaining floors used as the watch and lantern rooms. The light was automated in 1953.

INNER LIGHT, SAYBROOK, CONN.

LYNDE POINT (INNER SAYBROOK) LIGHTHOUSE, OLD SAYBROOK. In 1838, a 65-foot octagonal brownstone tower was built to replace the 1802 light at the entrance to the Connecticut River. The tower was painted white over the red brick, and on every floor, a window faced toward the water, giving it a distinctive look. In 1857, work began on a new keeper's residence in the Gothic Revival, gambrel-roof style, and a fourth-order Fresnel lens was added to the lantern room. By 1890, it was necessary to replace the lens with a less-intense fifth-order lens. The Coast Guard had the keeper's dwelling torn down in 1966, and the light was automated in 1975.

Inner Light House, Saybrook, Conn.

LIGHT HOUSE
STAMFORD, CONN.
STAMFORD HARBOR LIGHT, OLD GREENWICH, CONN.

STAMFORD HARBOR LIGHTHOUSE, STAMFORD. In 1881, a spark plug–style light was built on Chatham Rocks in Stamford Harbor with a cast-iron tower on a cast-iron cylindrical caisson foundation. Many keepers complained that the living quarters were not adequate for them and their families, so most lived in town and made the trip by boat. The light was decommissioned in 1953. Plans to use the discarded light as a historical site fell through, and it was put up for private auction. Over the next few years, the light saw a number of different owners.

WINTER AT THE LIGHTHOUSE, STAMFORD, CONN.

From Ella.

NEW LONDON HARBOR (PEQUOT) LIGHTHOUSE, NEW LONDON. With a number of lighthouses on Long Island Sound near New London, the Pequot Avenue Light, as it was known, was the first light built in the area. The year 1761 saw the first light, with a replacement in 1800. On a foundation of mixed stone, the octagonal tapering 90-foot-tall tower has thick stone walls with a lining of brick. In 1857, a fourth-order Fresnel lens replaced the oil lamps and reflectors, offering a visibility of 15 miles. In 1863, a new wood-frame two-and-a-half-story gabled-roof keeper's dwelling was built. The house was expanded to make additional quarters available for assistant keepers by 1900. The light was automated in 1912, and the keeper's residence sold to private owners.

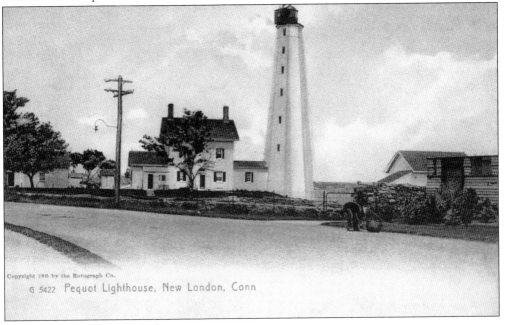

Copyright 1905 by the Rotograph Co.
G 5422 Pequot Lighthouse, New London, Conn

Sperry Light,
New Haven, Conn.

NEW HAVEN OUTER BREAKWATER LIGHTHOUSE, NEW HAVEN. At the west entrance to the New Haven Harbor in 1899, a cast-iron caisson was placed and secured, a cylinder put in place, and a cast-iron structure placed on the caisson. For added protection around the caisson, 13,000 tons of granite riprap were placed around the structure. A fourth-order Fresnel lens was used in the lantern room until 1903, when a second-order lens was used. The light was soon nicknamed "Sperry Light" after Rep. Nehemiah Day Sperry, who had been helpful in securing improvements for the harbor. With the caisson cracking and unable to be repaired in 1933, the light was decommissioned. After a new skeleton light tower was in place, the old light was torn down.

Sperry Light & Breakwater, New Haven Conn

Stonington
Light House,
Stonington, Conn.

STONINGTON HARBOR LIGHTHOUSE, STONINGTON. In 1840, after the previous light was no longer safe or effective, a new one-and-a-half-story keeper's house was built using stones from the previous light, with a 35-foot octagonal tower centered on the front of the house. In 1855, a sixth-order Fresnel lens replaced the lamps and reflectors. In 1889, the light was deactivated. In 1925, the lighthouse was offered for sale, and it was purchased by the Stonington Historical Society, with plans for refurbishing and using it as a museum. Below is a pre–1907 postcard on which the writer could only use the front of the card for their message.

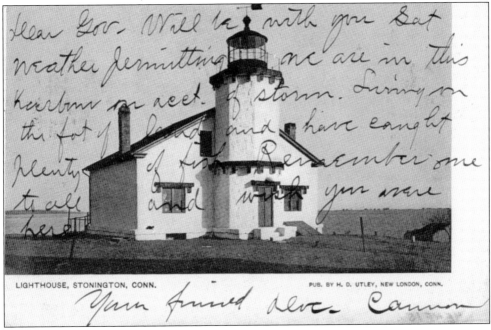

LIGHTHOUSE, STONINGTON, CONN.

PUB. BY H. D. UTLEY, NEW LONDON, CONN.

Old Light House. Light House Point, New Haven, Conn.

FIVE MILE POINT LIGHTHOUSE, NEW HAVEN. The first light tower at Five Mile Point, named because it is five miles from New Haven, was built in 1805. In 1845, a new tower was built to the height of 65 feet, with granite steps leading to the lantern room. The tower was also given a coat of white paint. By 1855, a fourth-order Fresnel lens replaced the lamps and reflectors. An enclosed wooden walkway was built to connect the tower to the new two-story brick keeper's house. In 1877, after the light at Southwest Ledge was lit, Five Mile Point became obsolete. The light and property were taken care of by the State of Connecticut and the Town of New Haven, and in 1949, the public was welcomed to Lighthouse Point Park.

OLD LIGHT HOUSE, NEW HAVEN HARBOR.

GREENS LEDGE LIGHTHOUSE, NORWALK. In 1899, Sheffield Island was known for the dangerous shoal that extended from the island into the harbor. Work began on a cast-iron, 39-foot-tall cylinder on a foundation. The tower is 32 feet tall and divided into four floors. The lantern room housed a fourth-order Fresnel lens. The light was automated in 1972.

Green's Reef Light, Norwalk Harbor, Conn.

Oct 13-06
E

Peck's Ledge Light, Long Island Sound.

PECK LEDGE LIGHTHOUSE, NORWALK. Peck Ledge Lighthouse helped marine traffic at the northeast end of the Norwalk Islands, while Greens Ledge helped the southwest traffic. In 1905, the cast-iron cylinder used for the foundation was filled with concrete, where a cast-iron structure was placed on the foundation, and with the added lantern room holding a fourth-order Fresnel lens, its height was 65 feet. The structure had three floors of living space and storage. The light was automated in 1933.

93

GREAT CAPTAIN ISLAND LIGHTHOUSE, GREENWICH. In 1868, a second lighthouse was built on Great Captain Island in a schoolhouse style, with the keeper's house made of granite and stone and a cast-iron tower on one end of the roof. An 1858 fourth-order Fresnel lens was transferred into the new lantern room. A fog signal building was added in 1890. The light was deactivated in 1970 and replaced with a steel tower. After the Coast Guard left the island, the town officials hired a caretaker for the light to ward off vandals. The island was sold numerous times over the ensuing years. By the 1990s, a campaign was started for a restoration project for the lantern room and keeper's quarters.

Great Captain Island Light, Long Island Sound, Conn.

Six

New York

OLD FIELD LIGHTHOUSE, NEAR PORT JEFFERSON, LONG ISLAND, N. Y.

OLD FIELD POINT LIGHTHOUSE. SETAUKET, 1823. Rocky shoals and sandy reefs were well known in the area around Long Island Sound in the early 1800s. In 1823, an octagonal 30-foot stone tower was built with a five-room, one-and-a-half-story keeper's house a small distance away. The light was a multi-lamp reflector with a visibility of 13 miles.

OLD FIELD POINT LIGHTHOUSE, SETAUKET. By 1855, a fourth-order Fresnel lens was installed in the tower. In 1869, a Victorian Gothic Revival–style two-story granite dwelling with walls two feet thick and a 50-foot height was constructed with a 28-foot, square cast-iron tower on the roof. The circular lantern room held the fourth-order lens used in the original tower. The keeper's area had living and dining space with a kitchen on the first floor. Bedrooms and a bath were on the second floor. A steel tower with a beacon replaced the Old Field Point Light, and in 1933, it was deactivated. The Village of Old Field used the property for a public park. In 1963, the original keeper's house from the 1823 light became the village hall.

Sands Point Light House, Port Washington. L. I.

We arrived here last night — all well — we had stormy weather last night but it's all right now. Harry

A. VAN WICKLEN, MAIN ST.

SANDS POINT LIGHTHOUSE, SANDS POINT. The Sands Point Lighthouse was built to warn mariners of the dangerous Execution Rocks just north of the point in 1806. The 40-foot brownstone octagonal tower had a wood-frame keeper's house. In 1856, a fifth-order Fresnel lens was installed, but within eight years, the old lantern room was in need of replacement. With the refurbishing of the windows, stairs, and the other buildings in 1867, a new brick framed keeper's house was attached to the tower. It was deactivated in 1894 but soon reactivated again in 1895. When a steel tower was put in place in 1922, the Sands Point Lighthouse was deactivated for good. It was sold at auction a number of times; now surrounded by private property, it can only be seen from the water.

Sands Point Light Station, Port Washington, L. I.

Red Bank Light House, Prince Bay.   Staten Island, N. Y.

PUBL. BY
W. J. GRIMSHAW

PRINCES BAY LIGHTHOUSE, STATEN ISLAND. In 1826, a lighthouse was built on the cliffs 85 feet above Princes Bay. In 1864, the complex known as the Red Bank Lighthouse replaced the earlier wood lighthouse with an Italianate-style two-story brownstone keeper's house and connected tower with a 15-foot passageway. It soon received a fourth-order Fresnel lens with a flashing white light. The light was decommissioned in 1922.

5284   CEDAR ISLAND LIGHTHOUSE, SAG HARBOR, L. I.   PUBL. BY WILLIAM M. COOK

CEDAR ISLAND LIGHTHOUSE, EAST HAMPTON. The Hurricane of 1938 turned Cedar Island into a peninsula. In 1858, the original lighthouse was replaced with a Victorian Gothic–style dwelling on a granite block pier. The L-shaped dwelling had a square attached tower with an 1855 sixth-order Fresnel lens. A skeletal tower replaced the lighthouse in 1934 and it was sold at auction.

FIRE ISLAND LIGHTHOUSE, ROBERT MOSES STATE PARK. By 1857, the 1826 light was found to be inadequate because of its low height and lack of visibility. A large keeper's dwelling and replacement light were built in 1858 with a 168-foot tower, using the stone from the original tower for the base and granite from New York for the dwelling. Handmade bricks for the new tower were covered in a protective cement coating in a cream color. The new tower was fitted with a first-order Fresnel lens. In 1891, the lighthouse was given its present distinctive alternating black and white stripes. In 1912, due to a crack in the tower, it was wrapped in iron bands and steel mesh and coated with a layer of cement. The light was decommissioned in 1973.

FIRE ISLAND LIGHT HOUSE, FIRE ISLAND, N.Y

Light House, Gull Island, New York.

LITTLE GULL ISLAND, SOUTHOLD, SUFFOLK COUNTY. Finding that the rocky reefs surrounding Little Gull Island helped with erosion control, in 1867, a grey granite tower 81 feet tall was built to replace the original light. A three-story Second Empire–style granite keeper's dwelling with a mansard roof was added to the complex. A second-order Fresnel lens was fitted in the lantern room. The station was automated in 1972.

STEPPING STONES LIGHTHOUSE, LONG ISLAND SOUND. In 1877, a Second Empire–style lighthouse one-and-a-half-stories tall was built on Stepping Stones Reef. The keeper's redbrick dwelling had a mansard roof and an attached square tower with a black cast-iron lantern room fitted with a fifth-order Fresnel lens. In 2016, a grant from the National Park Service helped to restore the structure. The Stepping Stones Light is still an aid to navigation today.

The Stepping Stone Light, L. I.

STATUE OF LIBERTY LIGHTHOUSE, BEDLOE ISLAND. Bedloe Island was a 12-acre island used as a navigational aid for ships entering New York Harbor. The statue was made of an iron skeleton covered with copper skin, sitting on a granite foundation. In order for the lights to be seen, two rows of circular windows were added to the copper-covered flame. The designer of the light, Frederic Bartholdi, had not thought about how to light the statue when it was dedicated in 1886. The torch rose 305 feet above sea level, and nine electric lamps could be seen 24 miles out to sea. In 1902, the statue was no longer an active aid for navigation and is now in the hands of the National Park Service.

LIBERTY ENLIGHTENING THE WORLD

RIGHT ARM LENGTH 42 FT.

12 PERSONS CAN STAND IN TORCH

DISTANCE BETWEEN THE EYES 2 FT. 6 IN.

40 PERSONS CAN STAND IN THE HEAD

LENGTH OF NOSE 4 FT. 6 IN.

WIDTH OF MOUTH 3 FEET

TABLET LENGTH 23 FT. 7 IN. WIDTH 13 FT 7 IN.

TOTAL HEIGHT 301 FT. 3 IN.

THE STATUE WEIGHS 450,000 POUNDS

STATUE of LIBERTY NATIONAL MONUMENT
BEDLOE'S ISLAND, NEW YORK   AARON HILL

LIGHTHOUSE - MONTAUK POINT, L. I.

MONTAUK POINT LIGHTHOUSE, MONTAUK. In 1796, a 78-foot-tall octagonal tower was built with red Connecticut sandstone and given a coat of white paint. A cast-iron lantern room with a copper ventilator was fitted on the tower to hold a first-order Fresnel lens. In 1860, the tower was raised 14 feet, and a new lantern room with iron steps leading to the light and a larger two-story keeper's dwelling were added. By 1899, a reddish-brown band was painted around the middle of the tower to make its daymark more distinctive. By the 1960s, erosion was becoming a problem for the tower, and the Coast Guard needed to act to keep the light from toppling into the ocean with only 50 feet to spare. In 1987, the light was automated. The 110-foot tower still stands today thanks to the Montauk Historical Society.

MONTAUK POINT LIGHT AND TURTLE COVE, LONG ISLAND, N.Y.

Execution Light House on L. I. Sound
Port Washington, L. I.

EXECUTION ROCKS LIGHT, LONG ISLAND SOUND. In the middle of Long Island Sound sits Execution Rocks Lighthouse, built in 1849; the tower was 58 feet tall with 15 lamps and reflectors. In 1856, a fourth-order Fresnel lens was fitted in the lantern room. It was not until 1867 that work began on a two-and-a-half-story granite keeper's dwelling. In 1898, a covered walkway between the fog signal building and the dwelling was finished. The tower was painted white until 1899, when a brown band was added midway up. In 1918, a fire caused damage to the engine house and part of the tower, but restoration of the light began immediately. The light was automated in 1979.

Execution Light House off Larchmont, N. Y.

Halletts Point, East River (Hell Gate) N.Y.

HELL GATE LIGHTHOUSE, ASTORIA. At the entrance to Hell Gate Passage is a hazardous area between the East River and western Long Island Sound at Hallet's Point. A tower was built in 1889, 15 square feet at the base with a height of 25 feet, built of wood. This tower replaced a metal light tower first used in 1884 that was too bright for marine traffic.

THE LIGHT HOUSE   SOUTHOLD, LONG ISLAND, N.Y.

HORTON POINT LIGHTHOUSE, SOUTHOLD. In 1853, mariners found a need for a light between the Old Field Light and Plum Island. In 1857, a 59-foot square tower with a detached two-story keeper's dwelling was built out of New England granite. In 1870, extra rooms for an assistant keeper were built between the house and the tower, connecting the two. The light was automated in 1933.

Eaton's Neck Lighthouse, L.I.

EATON'S NECK LIGHTHOUSE, NORTHPORT. In 1799, a 73-foot lighthouse was built at Eaton's Neck. Constructed from hammer-dressed freestone, the octagonal tower tapers from 18 feet at the base to 10 feet at the top. When originally built, the tower had black and white horizontal stripes; by 1854, it was painted all white. A one-and-a-half-story keeper's dwelling was attached to the tower by a covered passageway. At the same time, the lantern rooms were enlarged to hold a third-order Fresnel lens. In 1969, the keeper's dwelling was torn down when the Coast Guard took on the light. The light was saved from demolition when it was listed in the National Register of Historic Places in 1973.

EATON'S NECK LIGHT HOUSE, NORTHPORT, LONG ISLAND, N.Y.

LIGHT HOUSE, SAUGERTIES, N.Y.
Photo by LaRocca Studio, Malden N.Y.

SAUGERTIES LIGHTHOUSE, SAUGERTIES. A fire in 1848 destroyed the original 1835 light here, and a new one was built in 1850. Erosion necessitated a replacement light closer to the shore, where a circular granite foundation was to hold the two-story lighthouse. The tower was fitted with a sixth-order Fresnel lens. Electricity was brought to the light in the 1940s along with some modern renovations, like steam heat, plumbing, and a telephone. The light was automated in 1954. It was listed in the National Register of Historic Places in 1978, and the Saugerties Lighthouse Conservancy was started to help renovate the light; today, it is part of a nature preserve.

The Light House, Saugerties, N.Y.

HUDSON-ATHENS LIGHTHOUSE, HUDSON. A lighthouse was constructed in 1874 on a sandy ridge called Middle Ground Flats between Hudson and Athens. A Second Empire–style brick dwelling with a mansard roof was placed on a granite foundation. The light tower, which holds a sixth-order Fresnel lens, is centered on the western face of the redbrick eight-room dwelling. The light was automated in 1949.

HUNTINGTON HARBOR, LONG ISLAND. The original lighthouse was constructed in 1857 on the southern tip of Lloyd's Neck. The two-story wood-frame dwelling was built on a brick foundation, with the light tower attached to one corner of the building. A fifth-order Fresnel lens was fitted in the lantern room. It was no longer used after 1912.

9105 The Light House, Tarrytown. N. Y.

TARRYTOWN LIGHTHOUSE, SLEEPY HALLOW. In 1883, a conical steel spark plug–style lighthouse was built on the east side of the Hudson River. The 48-foot tower has five levels, with the first used as living quarters with kitchen and dining areas. Bedrooms were on the next two floors, with another floor for mechanical purposes. Eight porthole windows are spaced around the fourth floor. The lantern room held a fourth-order Fresnel lens. The foundation is a cast-iron caisson on a stone pier. For most of its life, the color scheme was a white tower, red pier, and black lantern room. When the east shore of the Hudson River was expanded, there was only 50 feet between the lighthouse and the shore. The light was deactivated in 1965. The refurbished light was opened to the public in 1983.

The Lighthouse and Hudson River, Tarrytown, N. Y.

SHINNECOCK LIGHTHOUSE, LONG ISLAND.
In 1858, a 168-foot redbrick tower was built at Great West Bay on the south side of Long Island. It is estimated that nearly 800,000 bricks were used. A two-and-a-half-story keeper's dwelling was built on each side of the tower, with one for the head keeper and the assistant keepers sharing the other; a covered walkway connected the tower and dwellings. A set of circular iron stairs provided access to the lantern room and the first-order Fresnel lens with a visibility of 18 miles. The name was changed from Great West Bay Lighthouse to Shinnecock Bay Lighthouse in 1893. In 1931, the light was deactivated. In 1948, the Coast Guard removed some bricks and replaced them with timber, which was set on fire, causing the tower to collapse.

SHINNECOCK LIGHT HOUSE, L. I.

U. S. COAST GUARD STATION & LIGHTHOUSE - HAMPTON BAYS, L. I., N. Y.

RONDOUT CREEK LIGHTHOUSE, KINGSTON. After two previous lighthouses on Rondout Creek in 1837 and 1867, a new lighthouse was built in 1915. The foundation was a reinforced concrete pier. The lighthouse, constructed of yellow brick, was a two-story dwelling with an attached square tower with a fourth-order Fresnel lens. The light was automated in 1954.

Orient Light House   Orient, Long Island, N. Y.

LONG BEACH BAR LIGHTHOUSE, ORIENT. In 1871, a two-story wood-frame keeper's dwelling with a mansard roof was built with a square tower with beveled edges on a screw-pile platform in the sandy soil of Gardeners Bay. A fifth-order Fresnel lens was fitted in the lantern room. In 1926, a reinforced concrete foundation was added to provide better protection from ice. The light was decommissioned in 1948.

110

Seven

New Jersey

Sea Girt Lighthouse, Sea Girt, 1896. Along a section of the New Jersey coast is an area called Sea Girt, which is not far from where the Manasquan River flows into the Atlantic. The beach at Sea Girt just south of Wreck Pond was 38 miles between the Barnegat and Navesink Lighthouses, and the property for a lighthouse was purchased in 1895.

Sea Girt
Light House

SEA GIRT LIGHTHOUSE, SEA GIRT. In 1896, an L-shaped, redbrick Victorian keeper's house was built with an attached tower that rose above the roof of the dwelling. A fourth-order Fresnel lens was fitted in the lantern room. The revolving lens had a flashing red light. The Sea Girt Light was the last lighthouse built on the Atlantic Coast with a tower and dwelling connected as one structure. The light was deactivated just before World War II, and the lens was removed. The structure was used during the war by the Coast Guard as a station to watch for German U-boats. The following years saw the lighthouse used as the Sea Girt Library and a venue for meetings. Restoration of the light began in 1981.

BEACON BOULEVARD SHOWING COAST GUARD STATION, SEA GIRT, N. J.

HEREFORD INLET LIGHTHOUSE, NORTH WILDWOOD. The south side of the Hereford Inlet in the Village of Anglesea leads from the Atlantic to the Intracoastal Waterway. In 1874, a wood-frame Carpenter Gothic–style lighthouse with a 50-foot tower connected to the dwelling was built here. A fourth-order Fresnel lens was fitted in the lantern room with a visibility of 13 miles. In 1913, damage to the foundation during a severe storm led to the lighthouse being moved 150 feet west. It was deactivated during World War II due to concerns about German submarine activity off the coast. In 1961, the lighthouse was turned over to the Coast Guard. The light was vacant for almost 20 years, and when restoration began, the paint was returned to its original buff color.

BARNEGAT LIGHT. NEW JERSEY

BARNEGAT LIGHTHOUSE, BARNEGAT LIGHT. In 1857, a second light was constructed 900 feet south of the original tower due to shore erosion, which caused the original tower to fall into the sea that year. The granite foundation of the new tower had a conical tower with an inner cylindrical wall nine inches thick. The tower stood 163 feet tall and had a first-order Fresnel lens. Living accommodations were built at the base of the tower for the keeper and his two assistants. In 1893, a 20-room, two-story triplex was built for the keepers. By 1919, with relentless erosion, the keeper's house was demolished. Jetties were constructed at the shore to ward off the encroaching waves. The tower was turned over to the State of New Jersey in 1926. "Old Barney" was relit in 2022 after restoration.

Old Light House, Keansburg Beach, N. J.

POINT COMFORT LIGHTHOUSE, KEANSBURG. Keansburg had two lighthouses that worked in conjunction as a range marker: Point Comfort Beacon on Raritan Bay, and Waackaack Light on Creek Road. The Point Comfort Beacon was built in 1856 as a wooden, one-and-a-half-story, schoolhouse-type structure that served as the keeper's dwelling with a square wooden tower attached to the middle of the roof. By 1867, repairs to the kitchen and roof were needed, along with a coat of paint. In 1883, jetties were built because of erosion of the bank, and riprap was added to protect the foundation. In 1904, an additional 400 tons of riprap were deposited to help the jetties hold back the erosion. The lighthouse was destroyed by fire in the 1950s.

Beacon Beach Light House, Keansburg, N. J.

157—Absecon Lighthouse
Atlantic City, N. J.

ABSECON LIGHTHOUSE, ATLANTIC CITY.
A brick cone-shaped tower was built here
in 1856. The 171-foot-tall tower had a
spiral staircase with 228 steps that led to
the first-order Fresnel lens with a fixed
white light and 22-mile visibility. It is
the tallest lighthouse in New Jersey. Two
separate keeper's houses were built, with the
head keeper's house attached by a 30-foot
passageway. In 1871, it was painted white
with a 52-foot red band in the middle. In
1876, erosion became a problem, and jetties
were used to build up the shore. The light
went through a number of color changes
through the years, and although the state
went with white and red, yellow and
black was also used as its daymark. It was
deactivated in 1933.

Atlantic City, N. J.
Light House and Government Property.

Light House.   Cape May Point, N. J.

CAPE MAY LIGHTHOUSE, CAPE MAY. The third tower to light Cape May Point was a 156-foot tower built in 1859. It had a first-order Fresnel lens that was strong enough to light Delaware Bay. The tower was entered through a two-story structure that had an oil room on the first floor and storage on the second floor. A year later, two one-and-a-half-story dwellings with three rooms on the first floor and four rooms on the second floor were constructed near the light for the keeper and assistants. The Lighthouse Service automated the light in 1933. The lighthouse had been painted white in the 1940s but in 1994 was returned to its original coloring of a light-beige tower with a red lantern room.

Cape May Light House.

3633   Egg Island Light House, Delaware Bay, N. J.

EGG ISLAND LIGHTHOUSE, DELAWARE BAY. In 1867, the previous light station here had been taken down, and a new lighthouse was constructed. This lighthouse was made to stand on piles screwed into the river bottom. The keeper's dwelling was a two-story structure with an attached tower on the roof. In 1878, with erosion continuing around the light, it was moved 1,000 feet northeast. It was automated in 1921 and destroyed by fire in 1950.

LUDLUM BEACH LIGHTHOUSE, SEA ISLE CITY. The Ludlum Beach Light warned of a shoal at Townsend Inlet. In 1885, the keeper's dwelling was a white wooden one-and-a-half-story structure with a pitched roof; a square tower was added to the front with a fourth-order Fresnel lens. Decommissioned in 1924 and sold, it was demolished in 2010.

SANDY HOOK LIGHTHOUSE, HIGHLANDS. Mariners entering New York Harbor had to pass a hazardous low-lying area called Sandy Hook that stretches four miles into the Atlantic. In 1764, merchants in the area petitioned for a lighthouse. An octagonal rubblestone 103-foot tower was built in the low area of Sandy Hook. The British unsuccessfully tried to destroy it during the Revolution. In 1842, a third-order Fresnel lens was fitted with a visibility of 19 miles. In 1857, a brick lining was installed in the tower for extra strength, and in the 1890s, a large wood-frame two-story dwelling for both the keeper and assistant was constructed. In 1963, the lighthouse was designated a National Historic Landmark.

Miah Maull Shoal Light House, Delaware Bay

MIAH MAULL SHOAL LIGHT, DELAWARE BAY. Featuring a cast-iron cylinder for the superstructure and a caisson-style foundation, this lighthouse was constructed on the Miah Maull Shoal just east of the main shipping channel in Delaware Bay in 1913. The living quarters had three floors of living space for the keepers. A Macbeth-Evans fourth-order lens was fitted in the lantern room. The light was put up for auction in 2011.

WAACKAACK REAR RANGE LIGHTHOUSE, KEANSBURG. Guiding shipping into Raritan Bay, this light worked in conjunction with the Point Comfort Lighthouse as a range marker. The wooden beacon was built in 1854, and by 1894, an iron skeleton tower was constructed to a height of 106 feet as a replacement, with a second-order lens. In the 1950s, the tower was dismantled and scrapped.

BRANDYWINE SHOAL LIGHTHOUSE, DELAWARE BAY. On the north side of the channel just west of Cape May, in 1858, a network of interconnecting iron piles circled this lighthouse, whereas the dwelling was made of cast-iron plates bolted together and lined with wood. A third-order Fresnel lens was fitted into the lantern room. Two floors were used as living quarters for the keepers. It was torn down in 1914.

SHIP JOHN SHOAL LIGHTHOUSE, DELAWARE BAY. The Ship John Shoal Lighthouse started life at the 1876 Centennial Exposition in Philadelphia. After being exhibited at the fair, it was disassembled and shipped to the caisson foundation in Delaware Bay. It was then reassembled with Second Empire styling and a mansard roof, and a fourth-order Fresnel lens was fitted in its octagonal lantern room. It was automated in 1973, and sold at auction in 2011.

EAST POINT LIGHTHOUSE, HEISLER. In 1849, a two-story brick rectangular dwelling was built to hold a lantern room with a sixth-order lens in the middle. The keeper's quarters had two rooms on each floor. In 1941, the light was shut down. It was reactivated in 1980 after some renovation and opened to the public in 2017.

COHANSEY LIGHTHOUSE, DELAWARE BAY. The original lighthouse was built here in 1838. A second was constructed at the Cohansey Light Station in 1883, where a white wood-frame dwelling with green shutters was constructed, featuring a square black lantern room on the roof. The light went up for auction and was sold in 1913, but the sale was later rescinded. It was destroyed by fire in 1933.

Eight

DELAWARE

Fourteen - Foot Bank Light, Delaware Bay, Del.

FOURTEEN FOOT BANK LIGHTHOUSE, BOWERS BEACH. In 1886, a pneumatic-caisson foundation was placed on the seabed and filled with concrete. A two-story cast-iron house-like structure was built in the Classic Revival style on top of the base. Attached to the structure was a square tower with an octagonal lantern room housing a fourth-order Fresnel lens. The light was automated in 1973 after an electric cable was run from the mainland.

FENWICK ISLAND LIGHTHOUSE,
FENWICK ISLAND, DELAWARE

FENWICK ISLAND LIGHTHOUSE, DELAWARE-MARYLAND STATE LINE.

This lighthouse was built on an isolated peninsula in Delaware at the Maryland border. A lighthouse between Cape Henlopen at the southern entry to the Delaware River and Assateague Island lessened the 60-mile gap between the two. In 1858, a brick double-walled 87-foot tower was constructed with a lantern room fitted with a third-order Fresnel lens. A two-story wood-frame keeper's dwelling was also built at the same time just east of the light for both the keeper and his assistant. In 1878, a second dwelling was built for the keeper and his family. The light was automated in 1978 and was soon deactivated. Ownership went to the State of Delaware, and after restoration with the help of a support group, it was rededicated in 1998.

HARBOR OF REFUGE LIGHTHOUSE, LEWES. Partway between New York Harbor and Chesapeake Bay, an almost 8,000-foot breakwater was completed. At the southwest end of the breakwater in 1908, a white hexagonal three-story, 76-foot structure was built with a cylindrical iron foundation and a fourth-order oil light in the lantern room. In 1922, the Harbor of Refuge Light was rebuilt to a height of 140 feet. In 1978, the light was automated.

New Light Station, Harbor of Refuge, Lewes, Del.

DELAWARE BREAKWATER LIGHTHOUSE, LEWES. The east-end lighthouse was built in 1885 with a concrete foundation and a cast-iron cylinder structure with four stories for the keeper's living space and an octagonal lantern room. When finished, the tower stood 51 feet high, with a coat of brown paint and a black lantern room. After an electric cable was extended from the shore, the light was automated in 1950.

Delaware Breakwater Light, East End, Delaware Bay.

Cape Henlopen Light House.

Built especialy for Easter picnics Herbert

CAPE HENLOPEN LIGHTHOUSE, LEWES. The Cape Henlopen Lighthouse was built on a foundation on top of a sand dune. The 69-foot stone tower was built in 1767 and survived the British in 1777. The keepers had a two-story wood-frame dwelling with a wraparound porch. The lantern room was fitted with a first-order lens. Although built at a great distance from the sea, with erosion eating away the shoreline, the light was soon endangered. By 1897, the sand surrounding the tower was thought to be blowing away at a rate of three to five feet each year. In 1914, the Lighthouse Service found that the erosion could not be halted except at a great cost. The light was deactivated in 1924. In 1926, it collapsed into the Atlantic.

CAPE HENLOPEN LIGHTHOUSE

BIBLIOGRAPHY

Cape Gazette. www.capegazette.com.

Crompton, Samuel Willard, and Michael J. Rhein. *The Ultimate Book of Lighthouses.* San Diego, CA: Thunder Bay Press, 2001.

D'Entremont, Jeremy. *The Lighthouses of Maine: Kennebec River to the Midcoast.* Commonwealth Editions, 2013.

————. *The Lighthouses of Massachusetts.* Commonwealth Editions, 2007.

hereffordinletlighthouse.com.

historic-structures.com.

Illustrated Map & Guide to Maine Lighthouses. Rhinebeck, NY: Bella Terra Publishing, 2019.

Illustrated Map & Guide to Massachusetts & Rhode Island Lighthouses. Rhinebeck, NY: Bella Terra Publishing, 2015.

lakesunapee.org.

lighthousefriends.com.

Rezendes, Paul. *The Lighthouse Companion for Massachusetts, Rhode Island, and New Hampshire.* Windsor, CT: Tide-mark Press, 2004.

Trapani Jr., Bob. *Delaware Lights: A History of the Lighthouses in the First State.* Charleston, SC: The History Press, 2007.

————. *Lighthouses of New Jersey and Delaware.* Elkton, MD: Myst and Lace, 2005.

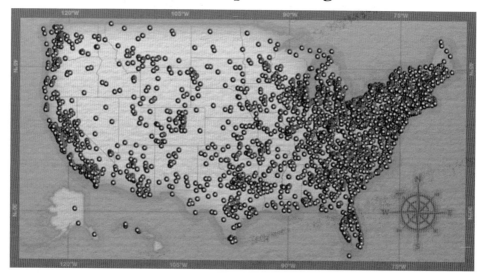